MICKEY
&
SAGE

Sara Farrington

BROADWAY PLAY PUBLISHING INC
224 E 62nd St, NY NY 10065-8201
212 772-8334 fax: 212 772-8358
BroadwayPlayPubl.com

MICKEY & SAGE
© Copyright 2014 by Sara Farrington

First printing: December 2014
I S B N: 978-0-88145-626-4

Book design: Marie Donovan
Page make-up: Adobe Indesign
Typeface: Palatino
Printed and bound in the U S A

ABOUT THE AUTHOR

Sara Farrington is a Brooklyn based playwright. She received her M F A in Playwriting from Brooklyn College with Mac Wellman. Sara is a HARP Artist at HERE Arts Center. Recent, upcoming and ongoing plays include CASABLANCABOX, a somewhat fake/ somewhat real making of America's favorite movie (HERE Arts Center, dir: Reid Farrington), LEISURE, LABOR, LUST, a 3-part play cycle exploring the world of Edith Wharton and old New York (JACK NY, The Mount, Lenox MA, director: Marina McClure), NEAR VICKSBURG, about love and war in the caves of Vicksburg (Incubator Arts Project, WalkerSpace, The Wild Project, Foxy Films), REQUIEM FOR BLACK MARIE, about the Brecht machine (Incubator Arts Project, Stella Adler Studios, Foxy Films), MICKEY & SAGE (Incubator Arts Project, ShelterBelt Theater, Foxy Films), THE VULTURES (Weasel Festival), THAT STAYS THERE (Bushwick Starr Reading Series), THE RISE & FALL OF MILES & MILO (FringeNYC, Winner: Outstanding Playwriting). Sara is the recipient of a commission from I R T Theater for her piece on the birth experience now and throughout history. Sara is a MacDowell Colony Fellow, Princess Grace Award finalist, Great Plains Theatre Conference participant. She studied theater at Connecticut College and The National Theater Institute at the Eugene O'Neill Theater Center. She has worked at The Wooster Group, was a resident actor at the former Jean Cocteau

Repertory, has toured internationally with husband Reid Farrington's work and held Broadway Play Publishing Inc together for many years, assisting Kip in his noble mission advocating for new plays and playwrights. Sara produces workshop versions of her plays at Foxy Films, a live/work space in Downtown Brooklyn. She and husband Reid have a son, Jack. For press, photos, podcasts and more on Sara visit: www.ladyfarrington.com.

The workshop production of MICKEY & SAGE was at Foxy Films Performance Space, Brooklyn NY, 10-29 January 2012. The cast and creative contributors were:

SAGE...Erin Mallon
MICKEY...Jack Frederick
HARVEY...Don Carter
MICKEY'S MOM..............................Megan Emery Gaffney

Director...Sara Farrington
Sound design...Sam Schloegel

The New York premiere was at The Incubator Arts Project, NYC, 21-20 September 2012. The cast and creative contributors were:

SAGE...Erin Mallon
MICKEY...Jack Frederick
HARVEY...Don Carter

Director...Sara Farrington
Scenic & lighting design...............................Cecilia Durbin

CHARACTERS

SAGE, *female, 9-years-old but must be played by an actress in her mid to late twenties, early thirties. 9-year-old* SAGE *never stops moving. She twirls, she kicks, she dances. She's very restless. 19-year-old* SAGE *is centered and calm, similar to young Sage but with the volume turned down.*

MICKEY, *male, 11-years-old but must be played by an actor in his late twenties or early thirties. He is aggressive, pent-up and angry, which is really a front for a scared and abused little boy. 20-year-old* MICKEY *is very much the same, but again, with the volume turned down.*

HARVEY, *male, in his forties or fifties. Should be played neutrally and sincerely, resist the urge to play him creepily. Trust and rely upon the sincerity of his words.*

VOICE OF SAGE'S MOM, *female.*

SETTING

The entire play takes place in SAGE's *fenced-in backyard.*

A tightly-slatted wooden fence flanks the upstage wall. There is a small, movable section of fence with two knotholes in it, perfect for spying on neighbors.

The back entrance to SAGE's *house is S R. The entrance is a screen door that makes a loud slap when it closes.*

There is an imagined or fully-realized window to SAGE's *mom's bedroom high up on the S R wall.* MICKEY *looks at this window often, terrified of his father.*

Place and time: An unspecific small American town now, then ten-ish years from now.

I.

(SAGE's backyard, late afternoon)

(At rise, SAGE sits alone. She is making a friendship bracelet from string tied around her toe. On the ground is a yellow Whiffle Ball bat, a baton and a brown paper bag.)

(Suburban neighborhood sounds are heard—cicadas chirping, an occasional distant car passing, distant voices, laughter, etc… They fade eventually.)

(A few moments pass and MICKEY enters. He's wearing a backpack. SAGE is excited to see him.)

SAGE: Hey Mickey!

MICKEY: Hey. (He goes to the bat and swings it wildly, aggressively.)

SAGE: What took you so long?

MICKEY: My dad had to stop at the drug store.

SAGE: (Handing him the bag) These're for you!

MICKEY: (Still swinging the bat, with no interest in the bag) What are they?

SAGE: Lisa Bergstrom's peanut butter crackers. She had 'em at lunch and when she wasn't looking I swiped 'em for you.

MICKEY: Oh. Thanks. But I have something better. (He drops the bat, reaches into his backpack and pulls out a bag of Doritos.)

SAGE: Whoa. Doritos?

MICKEY: My dad bought 'em for me at the drug store if I promised not to bother him and your stupid mom tonight.

SAGE: Whoa. *(Snatching the bag out of his hands)* Let's eat 'em.

MICKEY: *(Snatching the bag back)* Not now.

SAGE: Aw come on! I've never even tasted a Dorito!

MICKEY: Sorry Sage. These are for a special occasion. *(He carefully puts the bag of Doritos back in his backpack. He takes out a pair of binoculars.)* Let's spy. *(He goes to the moveable fence U S L.)*

SAGE: Other than Doritos, what'd your dad get at the drug store?

MICKEY: I dunno. Drugs.

SAGE: They don't sell drugs at the drug store.

MICKEY: Of course they do.

SAGE: Not the kind you're thinking of.

MICKEY: How do you know what I'm thinking of? Are you psycho?

SAGE: Psychic, not psycho. Like E S P. And no I'm not psychic.

MICKEY: What's E S P stand for?

SAGE: No one knows.

MICKEY: Hey look, Mister Neugebauer got another box delivered today.

SAGE: His house is filling up with boxes. My mom says he has a problem with buying things off the T V and internet.

MICKEY: We should sneak into his house sometime and steal them.

SAGE: Yeah! Let's do it now!

MICKEY: *(Matter-of-factly)* I would, but you're a bit heavy-handed.

SAGE: What's that mean?

MICKEY: It means you'd knock something over and he'd catch us and kill us.

SAGE: I could stand guard then.

MICKEY: You'd fall asleep or something.

SAGE: No I wouldn't!

MICKEY: We'd have to wait till Mister Neugebauer left his house. But since he never leaves I guess we're S O L.

SAGE: What's S O L?

MICKEY: My dad says it.

SAGE: Mister Neugebauer does come out when the mailman brings his boxes. I was sick with streptococcus A one time and I watched his house all day. I didn't even go to the bathroom. And when the mailman came, I saw Mister Neugebauer answer the door.

MICKEY: You actually saw him?

SAGE: Yep. And guess what?

MICKEY: What?

SAGE: He has a hunchback.

MICKEY: Whoa. *(He lifts the moveable fence from its spot U S L to a new spot D S L, flipping it around.)* Oh wow big surprise, Wilma McEleney's watching T V.

SAGE: Twenty four seven.

MICKEY: I like the show she's watching.

SAGE: *(With a jump to see over the fence)* Wheel of Fortune?

MICKEY: Yeah.

SAGE: My mom says that show's crap.

MICKEY: Well my dad says it a brain teaser show and if you watch it you'll get smarter.

SAGE: Your dad's blue collar.

MICKEY: What the hell does that mean?

SAGE: My mom says it all the time about him.

MICKEY: She does?

SAGE: Yeah, she says *(Dramatically, mock-sensually)* "Mickey's dad is so blue collar."

MICKEY: Well...he does have some blue shirts. Hey— you ever watched Wheel of Fortune?

SAGE: For the thousand millionth time Mickey, my mom and me don't have a T V.

MICKEY: Oh yeah I keep forgetting what a freak you are. *(Like he's in love)* Anyway, there's this girl on there and her whole job is just to turn letters and that's all she does.

SAGE: That's a pretty good job, I guess. That same time I had streptococcus A, the next day, I watched Wilma McEleney's house the whole day and all she did was watch soap operas. My mom says those are also crap.

MICKEY: Let's watch Harvey's house for a while. *(He lifts the moveable fence and links it up with the immoveable and fixed section of fence D S L, creating an L-shape. This is the way set stays for the rest of the play.)*

SAGE: My mom says to leave Harvey alone.

MICKEY: Why?

SAGE: My mom says he's in mourning.

MICKEY: What's that mean?

SAGE: Duh it means he only comes out in the morning. And since we're in school in the morning, it's pointless to spy on him now. Anyway his curtains are always closed.

MICKEY: That just means there's something going on behind 'em. (*He vigilantly stares at Harvey's curtains.*)

SAGE: So how long are you staying tonight?

MICKEY: Who knows—a year?

SAGE: I hope you sleep over again like last night and the night before that and the night before that.

MICKEY: I hope I don't. Your Strawberry Shortcake sheets are altering my D N A.

SAGE: That's impossible. Anyway they aren't Strawberry Shortcake sheets, they're Yakamoro All-Natural Bed Clothes.

MICKEY: Oh my God! Duck!

(MICKEY *and* SAGE *both duck.*)

SAGE: (*Whispering*) What?!

MICKEY: Shh!

SAGE: What happened?

MICKEY: Knotholes. (*He peers through the two knotholes in the fence.*)

SAGE: What do you see? Is it Harvey?

MICKEY: His curtains just...opened. Really fast, like this—whoosh. (*He reenacts the motion of the curtains with his arms.*)

SAGE: Can you see into his house?

MICKEY: Yeah. His kitchen.

SAGE: What's it look like? Is he in there?

MICKEY: No. (*He stands again, looking over the fence.*) You can come up, it's okay.

(SAGE *cautiously comes up. She looks into* HARVEY's *house.*)

SAGE: Ugh, his kitchen is messy and gross. He must not have a chore wheel. Did you get a look at him?

MICKEY: No.

(*Beat,* SAGE *is scared.*)

SAGE: I don't wanna spy anymore. I'm gonna go inside and see my mom.

(SAGE *heads off, S R.* MICKEY *intercepts her.*)

MICKEY: No no Sage you can't!

SAGE: Why not?

MICKEY: Because.

SAGE: Because why?

MICKEY: Because that's why my dad got me the Doritos numbnut. He said at the drug store that if we bug him and your mom again he's gonna take off his belt.

SAGE: What's wrong with his belt?

MICKEY: No no—

SAGE: Does he not like his belt?

MICKEY: You don't get it. (*Taking a new tactic*) Anyway, we're hanging out I thought. Just you and me. Maybe I will get to sleep over. That—would be—okay.

SAGE: (*Excited at the prospect*) Maybe we could make another toxic potion from stuff under the sink!

MICKEY: Maybe—sure. Just—don't go inside. Okay?
(*He turns his attention to spying on Harvey.*)

SAGE: I wasn't gonna bug them. I was just gonna get a snack. I'm starving.

MICKEY: Eat the peanut butter crackers.

SAGE: (*Hurt*) But—they're for you.

MICKEY: I have Doritos.

SAGE: Oo! Can we open the Doritos now?

MICKEY: No.

SAGE: Come on! My mom would never buy me Doritos in a zillion years. This could be my only chance to taste them!

MICKEY: Then it's best you don't.

SAGE: What?! Why not?

MICKEY: You'll never know what you're missing.

SAGE: Are they like White Cheddar Bunnies?

MICKEY: What are you talking about?

SAGE: Oh they're cheese crackers shaped like bunnies with cheese on them—only it's not real cheese. It's soy cheese.

MICKEY: Those're crap.

SAGE: They're not crap! Black seaweed crisps—those're crap.

MICKEY: If I gave you Doritos you'd probably run away from your abusive mother.

SAGE: My mom's not abusive!

MICKEY: I don't know Sage. All she ever feeds you is soy and rice and seaweed. They got better in the gulags.

SAGE: What's the gulags?

MICKEY: It's a Soviet stew made from bones and mud and throw up.

SAGE: Can you at least tell me what Doritos taste like?

MICKEY: They're amazing.

SAGE: You're so lucky. Your dad buys you good snacks. Maybe if your dad marries my mom, I'll get Doritos too.

MICKEY: My dad's not marrying your mom.

SAGE: Yeah he is. My mom said he is.

MICKEY: That's B S.

SAGE: Why's it B S?

MICKEY: Because my dad's already married.

(Tiny beat. This is a good moment for SAGE's *baton twirling to stop for a second.)*

SAGE: He is?

MICKEY: Oh shit! Duck!

*(*MICKEY *and* SAGE *both duck.)*

SAGE: What'd you see?

MICKEY: Knotholes. *(He again peers through the knotholes.)*

SAGE: Is it Harvey?

MICKEY: Yeah.

SAGE: What's he doing?

MICKEY: He's in the kitchen. Like, bent over the counter. I—I think he's…crying.

SAGE: Crying?

MICKEY: Either that or hysterically laughing.

SAGE: Gimme those knotholes.

*(*SAGE *pulls* MICKEY *away from the knotholes and gets behind them.)*

SAGE: He is crying. Mickey, why's Harvey crying?

MICKEY: How should I know? Keep your head down!

SAGE: He can't see anything. His head's in his hands. *(She rises over the knotholes and peers over.)*

SAGE: I'm kinda freaked out.

MICKEY: Be quiet.

SAGE: Mickey—!

*(*SAGE *suddenly ducks,* MICKEY *follows.)*

MICKEY: WHAT?!

SAGE: I don't know. *(Cautiously peering over again)* He's gone.

MICKEY: Where did he go?

SAGE: I think to another room. I don't like this.

MICKEY: I do.

SAGE: Anyway it's daylight savings time. It's gonna get dark soon. We should go play in my room.

MICKEY: I don't *play*, Sage. *(He watches* HARVEY's *house intently. Several moments)*

SAGE: *(With a kick to the air around* MICKEY*)* This is so boring.

MICKEY: You don't have a T V. I thought you were the one with the long attention span.

(Small beat)

SAGE: Hey Mickey.

MICKEY: What?

SAGE: Is that true about your dad? That's he's already married?

MICKEY: Of course it's true. He's married to my mom.

SAGE: Like right now, in your house, your dad and your mom live together and they're married?

MICKEY: Duh.

SAGE: Huh. Well—what's your mom like?

MICKEY: I don't know. She's kinda like Wilma McEleney.

SAGE: She watches T V a lot?

MICKEY: All day.

SAGE: What else does she do?

MICKEY: Nothing.

SAGE: Does she shop at the food co-op?

MICKEY: What? No.

SAGE: Does she subscribe to *The New Yorker*?

MICKEY: No way.

SAGE: Does she like vegetarian wok cooking?

MICKEY: I don't know—why are you asking so many dumb questions about my mom?

SAGE: I just wanna know about her.

MICKEY: She sits in her bathrobe and she watches T V.

SAGE: *(Sincerely)* Wow. That sounds great.

MICKEY: He's back.

(MICKEY and SAGE both duck. He peers through the knotholes.)

SAGE: What's he doing?

MICKEY: He's… Oh my God.

SAGE: What?

MICKEY: Sage…

SAGE: Tell me!

MICKEY: He's wearing a dress.

SAGE: What? No way.

MICKEY: He is.

SAGE: A dress?

MICKEY: Like a frilly Sunday church dress with flowers. And…oh my God…

SAGE: Urgggh what?! Tell me!

MICKEY: He's got a hat on.

SAGE: Like a baseball hat?

MICKEY: No, like…a lady's hat.

SAGE: But…why?

MICKEY: How should I know?

SAGE: Maybe he's rehearsing a play.

(Beat)

MICKEY: *(Fearful)* Sage.

SAGE: What?

MICKEY: He's…looking at me.

SAGE: But you're behind the knotholes. He can't see you if you're behind the knotholes.

MICKEY: Sage—he's…looking right at me.

SAGE: Let's go inside, Mickey.

MICKEY: I'm gonna say something.

SAGE: What?! No! Come on, let's make a toxic potion, huh?

MICKEY: He knows we've been spying.

SAGE: My mom bought a big bottle of ammonia-substitute at Whole Foods today. It's organic, but deadly!

MICKEY: He's a freak in a lady's dress. *(Shouting over the fence)* Hey perv! *(In one large movement, he leaps away from the fence, grabs the bat, leaps back to the fence and chucks it at* HARVEY's *window.)* Yeah we see you! We don't like perverts in our neighborhood, Pervert!

SAGE: Mickey!

(SAGE pulls MICKEY down.)

MICKEY: What?

SAGE: That's a horrible thing to say!

MICKEY: Are you kidding me?

SAGE: Harvey's not a pervert—he's an eccentric.

MICKEY: That sounds like something your mom would say right before Harvey locked you both in his crawl space. I hope you like baloney 'cause that's all you're getting!

SAGE: I'm sure he's just rehearsing a play!

(MICKEY *gestures toward the knotholes.*)

MICKEY: Look.

SAGE: I don't think—

MICKEY: Look!

(SAGE *peers through the knotholes.*)

SAGE: He's just…standing there. Staring at us. In a lady's dress.

MICKEY: Told you.

SAGE: (*Suddenly coming to her senses*) This is ridiculous. He's our neighbor!

(SAGE *stands up tall over the fence. Toward the end of this speech,* MICKEY *tries to break the baton over his knee.*)

SAGE: Hi Harvey! I'm Sage. I live next door, but you probably know that. I…ummm…I'm really sorry about what my friend Mickey just said. He's not even really my friend. He just gets dropped off here everyday for the past two weeks because his dad and my mom are…really really good friends. But Mickey's mean and his dad looks like a caveman with a hairy body. I hate him. I don't know why he's here or why my mom likes him. I never even ever wanted to spy. I think it's rude. You've got a right to do whatever, even in the morning, which I know you're in. So…consider this our last session. We'll never spy again. Or if we do, we'll skip over your house.

MICKEY: Great. Now what are we gonna do every day?

SAGE: (*Still standing, looking into* HARVEY's *house*) He's leaving.

MICKEY: Watch Wilma McEleney watch T V?

SAGE: He's gone.

MICKEY: If I'm gonna do that, I might as well stay at home.

SAGE: Where's he going? *(She slides along the fence to try to get a better view.)*

MICKEY: Spying was the only fun thing to do at your stupid house. I miss my house. I miss my room and my mom. I hate your mom.

SAGE: Don't say that!

MICKEY: I do! She's an idiot and she wears stupid necklaces and she smells like dirt.

(SAGE is about to burst into a rage at this, when the sound of a door slamming from HARVEY's house is heard. MICKEY and SAGE freeze in their action.)

SAGE: What was that?

MICKEY: Probably nothing.

SAGE: It was him. He's leaving his house.

MICKEY: That could have been anyone. It might not be him.

SAGE: When he kills us and buries us under his porch it'll be your fault!

(MICKEY runs to the door S R and peeks into SAGE's house.)

MICKEY: Sage he's talking to your mom. *(Beat. He watches.)* She's letting him in! He's here, he's in your house! Where's my dad? *(He calls up to SAGE's mom's bedroom window.)* We gotta get outta here. Dad! Dad! Let's go home! Please!

SAGE'S MOM'S VOICE: Sage!

(MICKEY and SAGE look at each other, unable to act.)

SAGE'S MOM'S VOICE: Sage? Mickey? Harvey's looking for you two.

(MICKEY *and* SAGE *scurry to the furthest corner of the backyard and cower.*)

(HARVEY *enters from S R through the door. He is not wearing a lady's dress and hat, rather, a typical middle-aged man's attire, ie: khaki pants and a collared shirt. He holds the bat that* MICKEY *chucked at his house.*)

HARVEY: Hi kids. *(Silence)* Shy? *(Silence)* No reason to be shy. *(Silence)* Playing a little baseball? *(Silence)* A little after-school pitch and catch? *(Silence)* The cats certainly have gotten your tongues. Haven't they? *(Silence)* Well. I'm just here to return your bat. *(He approaches the kids by a few steps, places the bat on the ground, and then walks back to his original spot.)* I'm sure you'll need it. *(Silence)* To hit those flyballs. *(Silence)* Better keep playing. *(Silence)* What with daylight savings time. *(Silence)* It'll be dark. *(Silence)* In no time.

(HARVEY *exits. Horrified silence from* MICKEY *and* SAGE.)

SAGE: Mickey?

MICKEY: Yeah?

SAGE: Can we open the Doritos now?

MICKEY: Sure.

(SAGE, *terrified and on the verge of tears, crawls to* MICKEY's *backpack, pulls out the bag and opens them. She eats a chip, savors it.*)

SAGE: Whoa.

(SAGE *is chewing, wallowing in the new flavor.* MICKEY *is still frozen in fear.*)

SAGE: These are amazing.

MICKEY: Sage?

SAGE: *(Mouth full)* What?

MICKEY: What happens to people?

SAGE: *(Mouth full)* What do you mean?

(Beat, MICKEY *considers what he means.)*

MICKEY: I don't know.

*(*SAGE *chews.)*

MICKEY: Hey Sage.

SAGE: *(Mouth full)* What?

MICKEY: *(Apprehensively)* You still wanna break into Mister Neugebauer's house and steal his boxes?

(Lights)

II

*(*SAGE's *backyard, late afternoon. Two weeks later.)*

(At rise, SAGE *is alone, dreamily playing with a Barbie. Next to her are a closed shoebox and two plastic shovels.)*

(The same suburban neighborhood sounds are heard distantly, with a few changes perhaps, a plane flying above, some kids playing, etc...)

*(*MICKEY *enters, a pack of Tropical Starbursts in his back pocket.)*

*(*SAGE *ignores him completely, focusing on bending and manipulating her Barbie.)*

MICKEY: Hey Sage. *(Silence)* Hello? *(Silence)* Earth to stupid girl. Come in stupid girl. *(Silence)* Wanna Starburst? *(Silence)* They're tropical. Here.

*(*MICKEY *tosses* SAGE *a Tropical Starburst. She doesn't snap out of it, doesn't acknowledge the object thrown.)*

MICKEY: Pina colada's the best. *(Silence)* I gave you a pina colada. *(He's had it with the silence.)* Hey! What's wrong with you? Usually you're like a ringleader in a circus when I come over. You're just sitting there looking at that dumb Barbie. What gives?

SAGE: *(Slowly coming out of her daydream)* Oh. It's you.

MICKEY: Duh.

SAGE: Where have you been?

MICKEY: What do you mean?

SAGE: You haven't been over in two whole entire weeks. Where were you?

MICKEY: I don't know.

SAGE: Oh my God sooooo much has changed. *(Temptingly)* Guess what?

(MICKEY *goes to the bat and swings it, ignoring* SAGE.)

SAGE: *(Even more temptingly)* I have big neeeeeews!

MICKEY: You're getting your vocal chords removed?

SAGE: Nope! I have a boyfriend.

(MICKEY *stops swinging.*)

MICKEY: What?

SAGE: Yep. Justin Bogart.

MICKEY: Who the hell is that?

SAGE: My boyfriend. I love him. He had to get his tonsils out and he stayed at the hospital for the past three days and ate nothing but tapioca and mashed potatoes and baby food. He's such a trooper.

(MICKEY *swings the bat again.*)

MICKEY: Phhff, that's nothing.

SAGE: Tonsils out is not nothing.

MICKEY: Three days in the hospital is. I had to be in the hospital for the past two weeks.

SAGE: What?

(The phone rings from inside the house.)

SAGE: Oh if you'll excuse me, the phone's ringing.

(SAGE heads for the exit. MICKEY runs to stop her.)

MICKEY: Oh Sage don't—

SAGE: But it's probably Justin Bogart!

MICKEY: But my dad said we have to stay in the backyard now.

SAGE: What?

(The phone rings.)

MICKEY: We can't come in the house at all anymore.

SAGE: But that's crazy, of course we can come in the house. It's my house.

MICKEY: Just let your mom get it—no Sage don't!

(SAGE bolts into the house. The screen door is about to slam with a crash just as MICKEY leaps to catch it, closing it very gingerly. He shoots a nervous look at the upstairs bedroom window.)

(MICKEY then wanders over to HARVEY's side of the fence and sneaks a quick peak through the knotholes. SAGE returns and MICKEY quickly goes back to swinging the bat.)

MICKEY: *(Innocently)* Who was it?

SAGE: A hang up. So why were you in the hospital for two weeks?

MICKEY: 'Cause I had an un-separated twin growing out of my neck. He was getting a little antsy so I got him surgically removed.

SAGE: Is that true?

MICKEY: Oh yeah Sage, it's true. His name was supposed to be Jeff but now I've got him in a jar next to my bed. And sometimes, if you listen real close, you can hear him screaming— *(In a squeaky, creaky voice)* Help me! Heeeelp me!

SAGE: You're lying. Why were you really at the hospital?

MICKEY: That is why. So have you seen Harvey since I been gone?

SAGE: No way, are you kidding? I don't even go near that side of the fence anymore.

MICKEY: I can't believe you and your mom haven't moved away yet.

(The phone rings again.)

SAGE: Oh if you'll excuse me—

MICKEY: Sage no come on—!

(SAGE exits into the house as MICKEY runs to catch the slamming screen door again. He closes it gingerly. He then looks back at HARVEY's side of the fence.)

MICKEY: *(Talking to himself)* I'd of moved across town by now. *(He spots the pina colada Starburst he threw earlier on the ground and cautiously tosses it over the fence.)* I'd of moved to Australia. *(He looks to the exit to make sure SAGE isn't on her way back. He looks over HARVEY's fence.)*

MICKEY: I'd of moved to the moon.

(SAGE re-enters, standing in the doorway. She, of course, catches MICKEY spying.)

SAGE: Hey!

MICKEY: What?!

SAGE: You were spying on Harvey!

MICKEY: Are you outta your mind? Don't slam the door!

(SAGE does.)

SAGE: You were!

(MICKEY looks to the upstairs bedroom window in fear.)

MICKEY: Please be quiet Sage, if my dad hears us he's gonna—

SAGE: *(Outraged)* I cannot believe you!

MICKEY: Listen Sage—

SAGE: I leave for one second and you almost get us killed again?

MICKEY: But listenlistenlisten, I know something about Harvey!

SAGE: You do?

MICKEY: Yeah.

SAGE: What?

MICKEY: You know how your mom said Harvey's in mourning?

SAGE: Yeah.

MICKEY: Well, do you know what that actually means?

SAGE: Yeah, it means he's an early riser.

MICKEY: No dingdong. I asked my gramma. It means someone he knows just died.

SAGE: Died?

MICKEY: Yeah.

SAGE: Who?

MICKEY: I don't know, you're his neighbor. Did you ever see anything weird over there?

SAGE: Other than Harvey in a dress?

MICKEY: Well yeah.

SAGE: Well, let me see. Oh! Last summer this guy used to come over and mow his lawn. It was really noisy and he didn't have a shirt. But then he stopped coming over. I don't know why. *(Gasp!)* Harvey killed him!

MICKEY: No, it has to be a lady. Did you ever see any weird ladies?

SAGE: Weird ladies?

MICKEY: I've been thinking about what we saw and here's what I think. Are you ready for this?

SAGE: Ready.

(MICKEY *paces the yard,* SAGE *close in tow.*)

MICKEY: Get ready 'cause this is a crazy theory, alright?

SAGE: Alright I'm ready.

MICKEY: *(Creating suspense)* Okay. I think—are you ready?

SAGE: *(Frustrated)* Urrrgggh I'm ready! What?

MICKEY: I think…Harvey killed some lady…and then…

SAGE: What?

MICKEY: And then…he put on her dress.

SAGE: *(Disappointed)* That's your theory?

MICKEY: *(Like a detective)* Now let me ask you. Did you ever see a lady? Hear a lady? Hear Harvey fighting with a lady, saying cusses at a lady, screaming at a lady, shooting a lady—things like that?

SAGE: Shooting a lady?

MICKEY: Shooting would be the best, if you heard that.

SAGE: No. I never heard any shooting.

MICKEY: Now think Sage, think really hard.

SAGE: I'd remember if I heard shooting. His house is actually pretty quiet. No one goes in, no one comes out.

MICKEY: *(Dejectedly, sitting on the ground)* Damn.

SAGE: Other than my mom being in the worst mood ever it's been pretty boring since the last time you came over. Although today she was alright.

(SAGE *gives a quick little air kick, then joins* MICKEY *on the ground. Mickey dejectedly picks at the grass.*)

SAGE: So what are we gonna do today?

MICKEY: I don't know.

SAGE: Oh! I have a surprise for you!

MICKEY: *(Disinterested)* What?

(SAGE slowly and excitedly slides her shoebox over to MICKEY.)

MICKEY: What is it?

SAGE: Open it.

(MICKEY does. He pulls out a bunch of Barbie heads with a single piece of string tied to each of their plugs of hair.)

MICKEY: *(Perplexed, a little horrified)* What do we do with this?

SAGE: Well you hate Barbies, right?

MICKEY: Yeah.

SAGE: Watch. *(She swings a Barbie head by the string around her head like a lasso, aiming it at the window above.)*

MICKEY: Oh no Sage don't—the window—!

(It's too late. SAGE has chucked the Barbie head, smacking the upstairs window. MICKEY has leapt to his feet and stands fearfully, looking up to the window.)

SAGE: *(Sure MICKEY loved this)* How about that, huh?!

MICKEY: Yeah great—

SAGE: You wanna try it?

MICKEY: No thanks—

SAGE: But I thought you hated Barbies! I did all this for you!

MICKEY: Thanks, but let's do something else.

SAGE: Wanna dig a really deep hole?

MICKEY: Sure.

(SAGE *starts dig.* MICKEY *just stands there, focused on the window, his back to her.)*

SAGE: My boyfriend, Justin Bogart, right before he got his tonsils out, he became by boyfriend.

MICKEY: What?

SAGE: Yep. He kissed me behind the multi-purpose room. On the mouth. So I'm really glad he's back from the hospital because I missed him. Because I love him. He was like, did you kiss anyone else while I was in the hospital? And I was like no! *(Small beat)* Even though I did. *(Small beat)* Don't you wanna dig, too? I have two shovels.

MICKEY: I'm okay. I'll just watch you.

SAGE: Suit yourself. *(She digs. About the digging)* Boy, this is fun. You're really missing out.

(MICKEY *is silent, still fixated on the window.* SAGE *picks up on his dark mood. She pauses in her digging.)*

SAGE: Mickey are you okay?

MICKEY: Fine.

SAGE: There's a virus going around at my school. Maybe your school too.

MICKEY: I don't have a virus.

(Beat)

SAGE: Well actually. Come to think of it. Now that you mention it. There was this really fat lady that used to stop by Harvey's house every once in a while with groceries.

MICKEY: *(Lighting up)* Really?

SAGE: Yeah. She'd come by Harvey's house in the evening in her car—a van actually. It was white. Everything was white.

MICKEY: What do you mean everything was white?

SAGE: Like she wore all white too. And she musta gone to Costco cause she'd have a ton of stuff.

MICKEY: Stuff like what?

SAGE: Oh you know, stuff—water, cans of stuff, white bread, apple juice. And…uh, *(Now lying to make it more interesting)* baloney, duct tape, knives, stuff like that.

(Beat, as MICKEY *blinks in sheer amazement. His fear has been forgotten for the moment.)*

MICKEY: Are you serious?

SAGE: Yeah.

MICKEY: Who was she?

SAGE: No idea. Do you think that could be something? Wait a minute!

MICKEY: What?!

SAGE: That fat lady hasn't been around in a while. Not in like, six months! Not since I turned nine! Huh. *(Resuming her digging)* Well, I guess Harvey just uses Fresh Direct now.

MICKEY: You're screwing with me.

SAGE: No I'm not.

MICKEY: You swear you're not screwing with me—you swear to God a fat lady dressed in white used to come by Harvey's house with weird groceries and now she doesn't come by anymore?

SAGE: I swear to God.

MICKEY: *(Excited now)* Okay. Okayokayokay. Okay. Okayokay. Whoa. Okay. I gotta ask you one more thing about this fat lady—

SAGE: Shoot.

(The phone rings again.)

MICKEY: Urggh. Who keeps calling you?!

SAGE: Probably Justin Bogart. If you'll excuse me.

(SAGE *heads for the exit.* MICKEY *intercepts her.*)

MICKEY: Waitwaitwait—

SAGE: I gotta get the phone, Mickey.

MICKEY: Let your mom get it, just tell me this—did she ever wear a church dress with flowers on it?

(*The phone rings again.*)

MICKEY: Well?

SAGE: Justin could be calling—

MICKEY: Did she?

SAGE: (*Just saying this so she can go inside*) Yeah, yes okay she did.

(SAGE *exits.* MICKEY *excitedly paces the backyard.*)

MICKEY: (*Forgetting to be quiet, going to the fence*) I can't believe you never told me this! Before we get the cops involved I think we should look for the body ourselves. My dad and me were watching this cops show one time and the guy on there was saying it's really hard to hide a body—he was like "killin's easy, buryin's hard."

(SAGE *returns.*)

MICKEY: Okay so the times you saw this fat lady—was she like really fat?

SAGE: Mickey.

MICKEY: Because that dress fit Harvey pretty good.

SAGE: Hey Mickey—

MICKEY: And you say she disappeared a year ago? Oh my God. Okay. The next step is to find the body, that's the next step—

SAGE: Mickey your mom's on the phone.

MICKEY: What?

SAGE: Your mom. She's on the phone.

(Beat)

MICKEY: Well—what does she want?

SAGE: She asked if you were here.

MICKEY: Shit.

SAGE: And I was like, duh.

MICKEY: What? You didn't say that.

SAGE: Of course I did.

MICKEY: But why?

SAGE: It's true isn't it?

MICKEY: That was a stupid thing to say.

SAGE: She thought so too because she laughed for some reason, like *(Doing a crazy laugh)* ah hahahaha! Like it was funny. Then she was like, lemme talk to Mickey.

MICKEY: Sage—

SAGE: You want me to tell her you're in the bathroom?

MICKEY: Nonono, I'll—I'll talk to her.

(MICKEY exits into the house. With chalk on the fence, SAGE draws a heart around the words "Sage + Justin." She sings as she draws.)

SAGE: *(Singing)*
John Jacob Jingleheimer Schmidt.
His name is my name too.
Whenever we go out.
The people always shout—
There goes John Jacob Jingleheimer Schmidt!
Dah dah dah dah dah dah dah.
John Jacob Jingleheimer Schmidt.
His name is my name too!
Whenever we go out—

(MICKEY *returns. His mood is again very bleak.* SAGE *tries to cheer him up.*)

SAGE: *(Cheery)* So! Where's the first place we're gonna start digging for that lady?

MICKEY: *(No longer interested)* I dunno. *(He puts on his backpack, sits and pulls out his Starbursts.)*

SAGE: What are you doing?

MICKEY: I gotta go.

SAGE: How come?

MICKEY: My mom's on her way over.

SAGE: She is?

MICKEY: Yeah.

SAGE: Like your mom's coming over to my house right now?

MICKEY: What are you—deaf and stupid? She was calling from the car. And she's not coming over, she's just picking me up. She's not coming in.

SAGE: Do you think—I mean, um. Should we tell my mom and your dad that she's on her way?

MICKEY: We're not supposed to go inside.

SAGE: Right. *(Beat)* Hey Mickey?

MICKEY: What.

SAGE: Were you really living in the hospital for two weeks?

MICKEY: I wasn't living there, I was just going there after school with my dad. That's why I stopped coming over for a while.

SAGE: Oh. *(Small beat)* But is there some reason why you had to go to the hospital everyday after school with your dad? Were you feeding soup to the homeless?

MICKEY: No.

SAGE: Were you singing songs to old people?

MICKEY: No.

SAGE: Do you have a secret job as a clown?

MICKEY: *(Suddenly terrified)* What? No!

SAGE: Well?

MICKEY: It was my mom. She got hurt.

SAGE: Doing what?

MICKEY: Acting like an idiot.

SAGE: Acting like an idiot doing what?

MICKEY: You act like an idiot all the time, why don't you ask yourself?

SAGE: Come on, tell me.

(Beat)

MICKEY: Does your mom ever spend, like, all the money she has on like, big pots and pans and dishes and clothes and, I don't know, shoes and candy and stuff?

SAGE: Uh…no. Well once my mom bought a sushi making kit and I've never seen her use it once.

MICKEY: That's not really what I mean. Does your mom, like, lie in bed for like, a really, really long time sometimes?

SAGE: No, my mom's usually doing chatarungas by five am.

MICKEY: I don't know what that is.

SAGE: Oh, I'll show you: *(She does a chatarunga, belly-flopping on the ground.)* That's a chatarunga. My mom taught me. Did you know she's a yoga instructor? She teaches your dad sometimes.

MICKEY: What?

SAGE: She's always like, "Mickey's dad is super flexible!" But not as flexible as me! Watch! *(She does a rough and sharp downward dog.)* Downward dog! *(She does a cobra pose, jarringly thrusting her chest forward into* MICKEY'*s face.)* Cobra! *(She does another downward dog.)* Downward dog again. *(She shoots her arms into the sky.)* Sun salutation! *(She lands in a mountain pose.)*

SAGE: And mountain pose. Nasty.

MICKEY: What?

SAGE: You always have to say Nasty when you're done with yoga.

MICKEY: *(Totally confused)* You're crazy.

SAGE: It's yoga, dum dum. It's fun.

MICKEY: You're lucky.

SAGE: Yep. Wait, why?

MICKEY: You have a nice mom and no dad.

SAGE: Well actually I do have a dad, but he's in India.

MICKEY: Why's your dad in India?

SAGE: My mom says he's finding himself.

MICKEY: *(Baffled)* What?

SAGE: It means he's super lost. In India, I guess, I don't know. I don't even really know him. But, yeah, I do have a pretty good mom. She's got her crazy things, though.

MICKEY: Oh yeah like what?

SAGE: Like she doesn't let me compost my homework even though my notebook paper's made from one hundred percent biodegradable materials. *(Swirling her finger at her temple)* She's crazy.

MICKEY: *(Disappointed)* She's not crazy. *(Tiny beat)* My mom took off all her clothes and ran out into the street.

SAGE: What?

MICKEY: Now that's crazy.

SAGE: *(Bewildered)* But—why did she do that?

MICKEY: She didn't like me getting dropped off at your house so much.

(A doorbell rings. MICKEY quickly heads for the exit with all his things.)

MICKEY: Gotta go bye.

(SAGE intercepts MICKEY.)

SAGE: Maybe it's Harvey though!

MICKEY: It's not.

SAGE: How do you know?

MICKEY: He's taking a nap in his living room. Go see for yourself if you don't believe me.

SAGE: Oh. Well, bye I guess.

MICKEY: Bye.

(MICKEY exits. SAGE, alone, goes back into her song and chalk. She writes "I love Justin Bogart" on the fence, near her heart.)

SAGE: John Jacob Jingleheimer Schmidt.
His name is my name too.
Whenever we go out,
The people always shout,
There goes John Jacob Jingleheimer Schimidt!
Dah dah dah—

(MICKEY rushes on suddenly, quaking in fear.)

MICKEY: *(Speaking quickly and fearfully)* Sorry Sage my mom just came in when I opened the front door.

(Both MICKEY and SAGE look to the door in fear as—)

(Lights)

III

(SAGE's *backyard, eleven o'clock at night. Several days later.*)

(*At rise,* MICKEY *and* SAGE *lie on their backs, side-by-side, heads nearly touching. They stare up at the night sky. He has on a short sleeved T-shirt. He also has a black eye and a cast on his wrist. She has on a long-sleeved shirt. She also has a Barbie lunchbox and her backpack near her on the ground. Some props from the previous act remain on stage, including the two shovels, Barbie doll, bat and baton.*)

(*Suburban neighborhood sounds are heard, only the nighttime versions, crickets, teenagers driving by blasting a car stereo, women on the street laughing, etc...*)

SAGE: Hey Mickey?

MICKEY: Yeah?

SAGE: Do you wear a watch?

MICKEY: Nope.

SAGE: So you're not a watch person?

MICKEY: Nope.

SAGE: What if you wanna know what time it is?

MICKEY: I never do.

SAGE: But what if you did?

MICKEY: I'd look directly at the sun.

SAGE: Ooo that's bad for your rods and cones.

MICKEY: What?

SAGE: Those are eye parts. I learned that at the Science Museum. We went there today on a field trip. Jessie Kalbacher forgot her permission slip. She has a hair lip. Have you ever been to the Science Museum?

MICKEY: No.

SAGE: They have a human head you can crawl into!

MICKEY: That's impossible.

SAGE: Well, it's plastic. I went in there with Brendan Hendricks.

MICKEY: Brendan who?

SAGE: Hendricks. He's my boyfriend.

(MICKEY *flips over, looking* SAGE *in the eye.*)

MICKEY: I know him. I thought Justin Bogart was your boyfriend.

SAGE: Ugh no way, vomit. How do you know Brendan Hendricks?

MICKEY: We played on the same soccer team in second grade. He's an idiot, Sage. You shouldn't talk to him.

SAGE: Brendan's not an idiot! He's my boyfriend!

MICKEY: That guy's a pig.

(SAGE *now flips over.*)

SAGE: Well then I guess I like pigs. He kissed me in the giant plastic head. Hey Mickey why do you have a broken arm?

MICKEY: *(Thoroughly disgusted)* You kissed Brendan Hendricks?

SAGE: Yep. I love him.

MICKEY: Sage—I cannot believe you kissed that guy!

SAGE: *(Playfully)* Jealous?

MICKEY: No! No I'm not jealous—it's just, I don't know. He's bad.

SAGE: He's not bad!

MICKEY: Yeah he is! One time at soccer practice I saw him spit into his friend's Gatorade when he wasn't looking and then his friend drank it and then Brendan laughed.

SAGE: Brendan Hendricks would never do that.

MICKEY: Well he did.

SAGE: Why do you have a broken arm?

MICKEY: It's not a broken arm it's a broken wrist.

SAGE: Why do you have a broken wrist?

MICKEY: I got it playing dodgeball.

SAGE: Oh. So what if you really really wanted to know what time it was right now?

MICKEY: I don't.

SAGE: But what if you did? You couldn't find out because it's nighttime and you couldn't look directly at the sun. You could look directly at the moon. Let's do that!

MICKEY: I already am. *(Beat)* Hey Sage.

SAGE: Yeah?

MICKEY: Didja ever notice there's a man in the moon?

SAGE: Hate to break it to you but I happen to know that man is actually a coincidentally composed formation of lunar seas.

MICKEY: You just happen to know that?

SAGE: Yep.

MICKEY: Don't act so smart, Wisenheimer. Just cause you go the Science Museum one time doesn't mean you're Einstein all of a sudden. I know it's not really a man in the moon, but it looks like one. You know what?

SAGE: What?

MICKEY: I'm obsessed with outer space.

SAGE: You are?

MICKEY: Yeah. Like you know what's driving me crazy?

SAGE: What?

MICKEY: Are you sure you wanna know? Because it might drive you crazy, too.

SAGE: I wanna know.

(MICKEY *goes to the fence and takes a piece of colored chalk.*)

MICKEY: Can I draw it on your fence?

SAGE: Sure.

MICKEY: Okay. There's the United States, right?

(MICKEY *draws the United States as best he can.* SAGE *sits on the ground watching him, like a student.*)

MICKEY: Then there's the planet Earth, right? *(He draws it.)*

SAGE: Yeah.

MICKEY: Then there's the solar system, right? *(He draws the sun with sunglasses and an expressionless line for a mouth.)* That's the sun. *(Drawing as he goes)* Mercury, Venus, Earth—that's us—Mars, Jupiter, Saturn, Uranus—

SAGE: *(Scoffing, as all kids do, at the planet's unfortunate name)* Phhhff Uranus.

(MICKEY *pauses in his drawing to give* SAGE *a disapproving look, slowly shaking his head at her immaturity. He goes on:)*

MICKEY: Neptune and Planet X or Pluto or whatever *(He draws Planet X as an "X".)* And beyond that is stars and nebulas and other solar systems and dark matter. *(For his depiction of dark matter, he draws as a small, three-dimensional cube. The drawing now huge and takes up a large section of the fence.)* But Sage, what's beyond that?

SAGE: Duh easy.

MICKEY: What?

(SAGE *takes some chalk.*)

SAGE: *(Drawing "more space," whatever that is)* More space.

MICKEY: Yeah, but what's beyond the more space?

SAGE: *(Drawing even more space)* Probably just more space.

MICKEY: Yeah but nothing can be just endless. And even if it was, what's after that?

SAGE: *(Drawing arrows out from the edges of "more space".)* More endlessness.

MICKEY: But after that?

SAGE: I don't know. God? *(She draws a big man with a beard.)*

MICKEY: But what's beyond that?

SAGE: Heaven! *(She draws a cloud with a heart inside it. Then she draws some small circles attaching the cloud to the mind of God.)*

MICKEY: That's B S. I want to be an astronomer when I grow up.

SAGE: What's that?

MICKEY: Someone who knows about all this stuff.

SAGE: That's cool. I'm gonna be an ice dancer when I grow up.

MICKEY: That's stupid.

SAGE: So if you were a watch person, what do you think your watch would say now?

MICKEY: I don't know.

SAGE: I'm guessing it would say...eleven seventeen pm. That's pretty late, isn't it?

(SAGE is now counting under her breath and on her fingers.)

MICKEY: I was up till one thirty A M one time. What are you doing?

SAGE: Eight and a half.

MICKEY: What?

SAGE: That's how many hours we've been in my backyard for tonight—eight and a half. Do you think my mom and your dad forgot about us?

(Both MICKEY and SAGE *shoot a look to the upstairs window now.*)

SAGE: Usually they let us in by now.

MICKEY: I know.

SAGE: Or at least bring us some food out. I think my body's eating itself.

MICKEY: Your body's not eating itself. You can go forty-two days without eating.

SAGE: What happens after forty-two days?

MICKEY: You die.

SAGE: Really?

MICKEY: Yeah.

SAGE: How long can you go without drinking?

MICKEY: Seven days.

SAGE: What happens after seven days?

MICKEY: You die.

SAGE: I know but how?

MICKEY: Your body gets crispy and dry like a Saltine cracker and you turn into sand.

SAGE: Whoa. It's a good thing I still have some rice milk in my lunch box. (*She goes to her lunch box, takes out her rice milk and hungrily drinks it.*) Want some Rice Dream?

MICKEY: I'd rather die.

SAGE: Suit yourself. Do you think we could just peek inside my mom's bedroom and see if they're in there?

MICKEY: No. You know the rules.

SAGE: Are we gonna sleep out here?

MICKEY: If we have to.

SAGE: That would be okay, I guess. Hey Mickey, how'd you get that black eye?

MICKEY: Dodgeball.

SAGE: Jeez, maybe you shouldn't play dodgeball so much. When you got here eight and a half hours ago, you said your dad said he was only dropping in to say hello and then you were leaving in a few minutes. Do you think he actually meant eight and a half hours?

MICKEY: *(Exasperated)* Do you ever stop talking?

SAGE: Maybe he did mean eight and a half hours. Maybe they're watching *Wizard of Oz*, that's a pretty long movie.

(MICKEY *tucks both his arms into his T-shirt, obviously freezing.)*

SAGE: Hey you want my sweater?

MICKEY: I'm fine.

SAGE: You're freezing.

MICKEY: I'm fine.

(SAGE *goes to her backpack and fishes out a sweater.)*

SAGE: If you don't wanna wear it because it's a girl's sweater it's not. *(She presents a very authentic 1950s button-down letter sweater.)*

MICKEY: Whoa. Where'd you get that?

SAGE: It belongs to my dad. He left it when he went to India. Because obviously you don't need a sweater in India, phhfff.

(MICKEY *puts on the sweater, but has a hard time negotiating his broken wrist through the sleeve.* SAGE *helps him.)*

MICKEY: Your family's weird, Sage.

SAGE: Not as weird as your family, Mickey.

MICKEY: I don't know about that, Sage. At least my mom and dad live in the same country.

SAGE: Phhff your dad lives in a cave.

MICKEY: Your mom lives in a hole.

SAGE: Your dad looks like Bigfoot.

MICKEY: Your mom's growing her armpit hairs for charity.

SAGE: Your dad got hungry and ate a sea cow.

MICKEY: Your mom ate my dad.

SAGE: Your dad ate the Empire State Building!

MICKEY: Your mom smells like dirt!

SAGE: Your dad smells like the sewer!

MICKEY: Your mom works in the sewer!

SAGE: Your dad swims laps in the sewer!

MICKEY: Your mom thinks two plus two is a million!

SAGE: If your dad had another brain, it would be lonely!

MICKEY: Your mom's the stupid one—she sat on the T V and watched the couch!

SAGE: We don't have a T V, stupid!

MICKEY: No wonder she doesn't know how to use one!

(SAGE *collapses to the ground, laughing hysterically at* MICKEY's *comebacks, muttering something like "you're so funny!" amid her laughter. He spots a visual disturbance first.*)

MICKEY: Sage.

SAGE: Oh I forgot to tell you!

MICKEY: *(Squinting his eyes at the fence)* What the—

SAGE: We still don't have T V, but we have the internet now!

MICKEY: What's that?

SAGE: Oh it's this thing on the computer where you can look up fun facts about kitties and ponies.

MICKEY: No—that.

(SAGE *looks, she freezes.*)

SAGE: Is it—?

MICKEY: Shh!

(HARVEY's *head pops up over the fence.*)

HARVEY: Kids?

(MICKEY *and* SAGE *scream and scurry to a far side of the yard. They cower, terrified.*)

HARVEY: Hey kids? *(Silence)* You still playing? It's eleven seventeen at night. Aren't nine-year-olds supposed to be in bed by now?

MICKEY: *(Outraged at this mistake)* I'm not nine you freak I'm eleven!

SAGE: *(Whispering)* Mickey shutup! *(A long silence)* Is he still there?

MICKEY: I don't know. *(To* HARVEY*)* Go away freak!

HARVEY: I don't know…I mean I…I'm not quite sure where I'm supposed to be at with all this.

MICKEY: What?

SAGE: Just don't talk.

HARVEY: It's been six months. What do I do now? I don't know how to do this. I—I don't know how to lose a wife. To have lost one. I don't know. After six months. Didja hear me? *(Silence)* She was there. And then…she…just…drifted away. I'm an accountant, you know. Accountants don't have many friends. But I had her. *(Beat)* Does that make sense? *(Silence)* Show some sign that you heard me. Please! Please show some sign!

(MICKEY grabs one of the plastic shovels and chucks it at the fence aggressively.)

HARVEY: Thanks. Can I ask you kids a question? *(Silence)* Are you kids home alone right now? *(Silence)* I said are you two kids home alone right now?

MICKEY: *(Whispering to SAGE)* Say no.

SAGE: *(To HARVEY)* Uh… No. My mom and his dad are upstairs watching *Wizard of Oz*.

HARVEY: Ah. Great film. You know Buddy Ebsen was slated to play The Tin Man, but of course lost out to Jack Haley.

MICKEY: Who?

SAGE: What?

HARVEY: Nevermind. Listen, Sage, I happen to notice your mom's car isn't in the driveway. And Mickey, your dad's Bronco was in the driveway at around three this afternoon, but it's gone now too. Been gone for hours. Do you kids have a babysitter?

MICKEY: We don't need a stupid babysitter!

HARVEY: Right, no, of course not. Well, I'm home. Okay? And uh. I don't sleep much at night—I guess you might call me nocturnal, huh? *(A little chuckle)* Anyway, are you two kids hungry? Did your parents feed you before they, uh, started watching *The Wizard of Oz*?

SAGE: *(To HARVEY)* I'm starving.

MICKEY: Shutup.

SAGE: *(To MICKEY)* But I am!

HARVEY: Starving?

MICKEY: *(To HARVEY)* We're fine! Go away!

HARVEY: I'll be right back.

Harvey exits. Mickey goes to the fence.

(MICKEY *aggressively mouths the word "FUCK!".*)

SAGE: Don't say that word!

MICKEY: I didn't say it I mouthed it.

SAGE: Don't even mouth it.

MICKEY: This is an emergency, I can mouth whatever I want.

SAGE: Is my mom's car really gone?

MICKEY: He's lying. He's trying to lure us into his perv dungeon.

SAGE: Are we really home alone right now?

MICKEY: Don't be stupid, it's a trick.

SAGE: I'm not allowed to be home alone yet.

MICKEY: We're not home alone.

SAGE: But what if we are? What if they're really gone? I'm gonna go check my mom's bedroom.

(SAGE *heads for the exit.* MICKEY *intercepts her.*)

MICKEY: No Sage don't!

SAGE: You said yourself this is an emergency.

MICKEY: But my dad'll kill me.

SAGE: No he won't.

MICKEY: He will! Please don't go inside!

SAGE: (*She's had it with his evasions.*) Why?!

MICKEY: Because…remember when you chucked that Barbie's head at the window?

SAGE: Yeah?

(MICKEY *lifts and lowers his broken wrist.*)

SAGE: But… I thought you said you got that playing dodgeball.

MICKEY: Well, I didn't.

(Beat, as SAGE tries to make sense of this.)

SAGE: Listen all I'm gonna do is sneak upstairs and put my ear on the wall. If I hear anything at all I'll run right back.

MICKEY: Please don't.

SAGE: Wouldn't you rather your dad kill you than Harvey?

(Beat, SAGE has a point.)

MICKEY: You have to be really really quiet.

SAGE: Obviously. *(She turns to go.)*

MICKEY: Sage wait!

SAGE: What?

MICKEY: Be really really fast, too.

SAGE: Okay.

(SAGE exits into the house. MICKEY catches the door and closes it quietly.)

(Ambient neighborhood sounds swell, crickets, teenagers blaring a car stereo bass, cars driving by, a pack of laughing women.)

(MICKEY is terrified. He grabs the bat for protection and sits on the ground. He starts to itch under his cast with his fingers. He soon buries his head between his knees, running his hands through his hair, miserable.)

(SAGE soon returns with a folded slip of paper in her hands. She halts in the doorway when she sees MICKEY in this sad state.)

SAGE: Mickey?

MICKEY: *(Head in still his hands)* Yeah?

SAGE: Are you okay?

MICKEY: Fine. Were they there?

SAGE: Do you think you have a virus? There's one going around my school and—

MICKEY: I'm fine. Were they there!?

SAGE: Uh… Maybe you should call your mom. Maybe she can babysit us.

MICKEY: Why?

SAGE: Because they're not in my mom's room.

MICKEY: Did you check other rooms?

SAGE: No.

MICKEY: Why not?

SAGE: Because Harvey's right. The cars are both gone.

(HARVEY's *head pops up again from behind the fence.*)

HARVEY: Hey kids.

(MICKEY *and* SAGE *instantly hit the ground, plunged into a deeper level of terror.*)

HARVEY: Here you go.

(HARVEY *presents a foil covered plate, holding it over the fence.*)

HARVEY: Go ahead. Take it.

(MICKEY *and* SAGE *don't move.*)

HARVEY: It's fudge. My niece left it on my doorstep. I'm never gonna eat it. Not really keen on sweets. It's all different flavors. Go ahead, take it.

(MICKEY *and* SAGE *don't move.*)

HARVEY: Alright well, how about I just…drop it over?

(HARVEY *drops the foil-covered plate [a paper plate] over the fence.* MICKEY *and* SAGE *kids flinch when it hits the ground,* MICKEY *grabbing the bat for protection.*)

HARVEY: There you go. Uh, kids, uh. If it turns out you are alone, I want to tell you—are you listening?

SAGE: Yeah.

MICKEY: Shutup!

HARVEY: Don't be scared.

MICKEY: I'm not scared!

SAGE: We're not scared!

HARVEY: Good! Because remember, you're not really alone, are you? You have each other. And if you have each other, you're not really alone. It's when you don't have each other. It's when one of you is gone. That's when it gets really scary.

(*Beat as* SAGE *looks to* MICKEY *for clarification.* MICKEY *is looking at* HARVEY *with suspicion.*)

HARVEY: Okay?

SAGE: (*To* HARVEY, *in a thin, scared little voice*) I—I don't know.

HARVEY: That's okay. No one does.

(HARVEY *exits. After a beat,* SAGE *grabs the bat from* MICKEY's *hands and cautiously approaches the plate.*)

MICKEY: Sage don't even touch it.

SAGE: Why? (*She pokes at the foil.*)

MICKEY: Because I saw this movie one time where this one lady gives this other lady a plate that's covered with one of those metal cover things and she's like (*Aping the voice of Bette Davis in* What Ever Happened to Baby Jane, *the movie he somehow saw and is somehow referencing*) "we got rats in the basement." And when the one lady lifts the cover there's a dead rat under there!

SAGE: What movie is that?

MICKEY: It's called "Rats in the Basement".

SAGE: Never heard of it. Anyway, I don't think it's a dead rat. It feels smushy.

MICKEY: Dead rats are smushy!

(MICKEY *and* SAGE *huddle over the plate. She lifts one corner of the foil up with the bat. She gasps first, then he gasps.*)

MICKEY: *(Averting his eyes)* Oh my God! What is it?!

SAGE: It's…fudge.

MICKEY: Well don't eat it.

SAGE: *(Overlapping)* Oh I won't. Poison.

MICKEY: *(Overlapping)* Poison.

MICKEY: *(Overlapping)* Yep.

SAGE: *(Overlapping)* Yep. *(She continues to investigate the fudge, without actually touching it with her hands.)*

MICKEY: You're sure my dad and your mom weren't in your mom's room?

SAGE: Sure I'm sure. Nothing was in my mom's room.

MICKEY: What do you mean?

SAGE: Like everything was gone. Her closet was wide open and like, half her clothes were missing.

MICKEY: What?

SAGE: Yeah and her shoes too. I also looked in her bathroom and her makeup bag was gone. And all her necklaces which she keeps on the bedpost? Yeah, those were gone too.

MICKEY: That's…but…why?

SAGE: I don't know. Yard sale?

MICKEY: In the middle of the night?

SAGE: *(Gasp!)* You think Harvey had something to do with it?

MICKEY: I don't know.

SAGE: Oh and also there was this taped to the front door.

(SAGE *hands* MICKEY *the note she entered with. He reads it to himself. Once he's gotten to the bottom of the note, he starts reading it again from the beginning. This should take a long time. When he's done, he crumples the note up in his fist and chucks it the upstairs window.*)

MICKEY: You know what we should do?

SAGE: What?

MICKEY: We should have Harvey eat one of these fudge things himself.

SAGE: Too late now.

MICKEY: That woulda been smart.

SAGE: Yeah, we could be eating these right now.

MICKEY: If they weren't poison, you mean.

SAGE: Obviously.

MICKEY: You say obviously a lot.

SAGE: You ever seen this movie called *The Princess Bride*?

MICKEY: No.

SAGE: Well there's a guy in there who's made himself, like um, where poison doesn't hurt you because like you're used to it, you know?

MICKEY: Immune?

SAGE: Yeah! By drinking a tiny little bit of it everyday.

MICKEY: Really?

SAGE: Yeah. So what if we took like, a teensy tiny teensy little bite of one of these fudge things and we did that every day for like a year, then, we could eat all of these and not die.

MICKEY: *(Considering it)* Huh.

SAGE: Yeah?

MICKEY: You're not as stupid as you look and sound.

SAGE: *(Taking this as a compliment)* Aw thanks Mickey!
So let's do it.

MICKEY: Okay.

SAGE: Okay.

MICKEY: You do it.

SAGE: You do it.

MICKEY: Ladies first.

SAGE: Be my guest.

MICKEY: But ladies first.

SAGE: But I'm giving you my turn.

MICKEY: But I don't want your turn.

SAGE: We have to do it at the same time then.

MICKEY: Okay.

SAGE: Okay.

*(MICKEY and SAGE each take a fudge square. He drops it
quickly as if it's burning.)*

MICKEY: OW!

SAGE: *(Dropping hers too)* What! What is it?

MICKEY: *(Picking up the square again)* False alarm.

SAGE: *(Picking up hers)* Oh. Ready?

MICKEY: Ready.

SAGE: Wait wait!

MICKEY: What?

SAGE: Just in case this is—you know—it, I want you to
know—I love you.

(Beat)

MICKEY: What?

SAGE: I love you.

MICKEY: *(Not knowing how to react to this sentiment so choosing annoyance)* Aw shit.

SAGE: What?

MICKEY: I don't know. Don't you have, like, a million boyfriends?

SAGE: I love them, too.

MICKEY: Oh.

SAGE: But if I had to choose, I'd say I loved you the most.

(Small beat)

MICKEY: *(Still annoyed, but also liking this, but mostly grossed out?)* Aw man.

SAGE: It's true.

MICKEY: Well. I guess that means I should say that?

SAGE: You don't have to.

MICKEY: Well. Okay I'll say—I always thought—that—for a girl, you're…fine.

SAGE: Really?

MICKEY: I guess.

(SAGE smiles, thrilled at this.)

SAGE: Now. Let's take a teensy weensy bite. Okay? Almost like nothing at all.

(MICKEY and SAGE each take a tiny bite and swallow.)

MICKEY: Well?

SAGE: What does poison taste like usually?

MICKEY: Burnt almonds.

SAGE: Really?

MICKEY: Yeah, I've heard that.

SAGE: This doesn't taste like burnt almonds. It takes like chocolate.

MICKEY: Yeah mine too. Maybe it's like, a slow moving poison.

SAGE: Maybe.

MICKEY: So in that movie, how much time does the guy taking poison take poison for to make himself immune to poison?

SAGE: That's not really addressed in the film.

MICKEY: Oh. So we just sit here and take tiny bites for a year?

SAGE: I don't see any other way, do you?

MICKEY: No.

(Beat, as MICKEY *and* SAGE *take another teensy bite.)*

SAGE: *(A sudden realization)* Hold on a minute!

MICKEY: What?!

SAGE: Fudge is a like a baked thing right? Like you have to put it in the oven or stove?

MICKEY: Uh, I don't know.

SAGE: Which means that even if these are poisoned, the heat from the stove pushed out all the toxins!

MICKEY: *(Skeptical)* Is that true?

SAGE: Heat kills toxins!

MICKEY: *(Still skeptical)* Was that at The Science Museum, too?

SAGE: Yeah, I'm pretty sure it was but I mostly know that because my mom always makes me wait at The Healing Center where they have no fun things in the waiting room except that baby's toy with the rainbow beads on the roller coaster thing—which is always really sticky anyway—while my mom's sitting in the stupid sweat room and when she finally gets out after like forty hours I'm always like "what took you so long?" And she's always like "I was getting rid of my toxins".

MICKEY: Are toxins the same as poisons?

SAGE: Obviously!

MICKEY: So can we eat these?

(A tense beat right before MICKEY *and* SAGE *dig in, devouring the fudge, in heaven.)*

MICKEY: *(Mouth full)* Oh Jesus.

SAGE: *(Mouth full)* Whoa. These are not carob.

MICKEY: Uh uh.

SAGE: This is real.

MICKEY: Uh huh. This one's coconut.

SAGE: Gimme that. *(She snatches* MICKEY's *coconut square and shovels into her mouth.)* Holy shit.

MICKEY: *(Shocked)* Sage! I've never heard you say a bad word before. I didn't even know you know 'em.

SAGE: Of course I know 'em! I know *(She mouths the word "FUCK!")*

MICKEY: Just say it.

SAGE: Oh no, it's really bad, it's like, the worst word.

MICKEY: Who's gonna get you in trouble? We're home alone!

(Small beat)

SAGE: Fuck fuck fuck!

MICKEY: *(Laughing)* Say shit.

SAGE: Shit shit shit!

MICKEY: Say shit shit shit tits!

SAGE: Shit shit shit tits!

(MICKEY *and* SAGE *are howling with laughter, high on fudge and bad words.*)

MICKEY: Say shit tits penis!

SAGE: *(To the heavens)* Shit tits penis!

MICKEY: Penis diarrhea!

SAGE: *(In ecstasy, as if to God)* Penis diarrhea!

MICKEY: Stupid diarrhea face!

SAGE: *(Same)* Stupid diarrhea bitchy bitchface ass!

MICKEY: *(Impressed by this turn of phrase)* Whoa Sage, that was really good!

SAGE: *(The biggest one yet)* Asshole face tits butt penis!

(MICKEY *and* SAGE'*s laughter peaks and they collapse on the ground. Their laughter tapers off, but then returns, like a wave, then tapers off again. It should take a long time to recover from the moment.*)

SAGE: Hey Mickey?

MICKEY: Yeah?

SAGE: Did that note sound like they were ever coming back?

MICKEY: No.

SAGE: I don't think so either. So I guess we're orphans.

MICKEY: They're not dead, numbnut. They're just stupid.

SAGE: I guess we don't have to stay in the backyard anymore.

MICKEY: Let's watch T V!

SAGE: Urgggh we don't have a T V, you idiot! But! We do have internet!

(MICKEY *is gripped by a sudden realization. He excitedly grabs* SAGE *by the shoulders.*)

MICKEY: THERE'S T V ON THE INTERNET! Plus all kinds of other shit!

SAGE: Like pictures of bunnies and baby kittens and a man covered in bees!

MICKEY: And naked ladies! And car accidents! And fat babies smoking cigarettes! And oh my God let's do it!

(MICKEY *and* SAGE *scramble to their feet and head for the exit. He leaves, but she remembers:*)

SAGE: Oh wait! The fudge! (*She scrambles back to the fudge, grabs it and exits.*)

(*Lights. In this transition,* HARVEY *enters with a bucket and sponge. He gathers all the items in the yard, the shovels, the Barbie, the backpacks, the bat and baton. He then wipes off* MICKEY *and* SAGE*'s chalk drawing of the universe on the fence with a wet sponge. When the fence is wiped completely clean, he gives the yard one last look and exits.*)

IV

(SAGE*'s backyard, late afternoon. Ten-ish years later.*)

(SAGE *is doing yoga. She is wearing long-sleeved bright red blouse. Much of the explosive energy she had as a kid has been channeled into her yoga practice.*)

(*Ambient suburban sounds are heard, same as before. They fade when the scene starts, same as before.*)

(MICKEY *enters.* SAGE *doesn't see him as he observes her graceful yoga poses. Soon, she spots him, maybe through an upsidedown position?*)

SAGE: Mickey.

MICKEY: Hey.

(*Beat*)

SAGE: What are you—? Hi.

MICKEY: Hi. *(Beat)* Your, uh, Aunt Margaret let me in.

SAGE: Oh. That's—good, yeah. Okay.

MICKEY: So.

SAGE: Yeah.

MICKEY: How are you?

SAGE: How are you?

MICKEY: Fine.

SAGE: Good.

(Silence)

MICKEY: How are you?

SAGE: Fine.

MICKEY: Good.

(Beat)

SAGE: Leaving in twenty minutes.

MICKEY: Yeah, your Aunt Margaret told me.

SAGE: Yeah. *(Beat)* I have to get to the airport by three.

MICKEY: She mentioned that.

SAGE: Oh. *(Beat)* Well— How are you?

MICKEY: Fine.

SAGE: Fine. Fine fine fine.

MICKEY: Yeah.

SAGE: Yeah.

MICKEY: I couldn't—come to your goodbye party last week.

SAGE: Yeah.

MICKEY: Sorry.

SAGE: Yep.

MICKEY: And I haven't...called you back in a while.

SAGE: Yeah no.

MICKEY: You're mad.

SAGE: *(Quick cue)* Oh God no not anymore no.

MICKEY: I was sick.

SAGE: What sort of sickness did you have?

MICKEY: I was!

SAGE: The flu?

MICKEY: I really was sick, Sage. I couldn't lift my head up.

SAGE: From out of the toilet?

(Beat)

MICKEY: Kyle Pearson didn't want me there.

SAGE: I don't care what Kyle wants.

MICKEY: He's your boyfriend.

SAGE: So?

MICKEY: He thinks I'm a scummer.

SAGE: A scummer?

MICKEY: What?

SAGE: You've got to stop hanging out at The Tavern. You're not even old enough to drink and you're already turning into your— *(She cuts herself off.)* So what do you want?

MICKEY: Are you coming back for Thanksgiving?

SAGE: Maybe. If I can afford a plane ticket.

MICKEY: You should.

SAGE: Why?

MICKEY: I don't know.

SAGE: Are you coming back for Thanksgiving?

MICKEY: Uh. Yeah. Well, I'll already be here.

SAGE: You will?

MICKEY: Yeah.

SAGE: Why?

MICKEY: Because I'm…not leaving.

SAGE: What?

MICKEY: I'm gonna take a year off.

SAGE: Since when!?

MICKEY: Iggy Potzdale's dad offered me a job at his landscaping company. I really like it there and the people are super nice. And I'll make enough money to move out of my gramma's house finally. Iggy Potzdale's working there, too.

SAGE: But Mickey—

MICKEY: What?

SAGE: I just—

MICKEY: What?

SAGE: What are you gonna tell the school?

MICKEY: Nothing.

SAGE: So it's money?

MICKEY: No—

SAGE: Because you can take out loans—tons of 'em! And the more of a sob story you give 'em the more money you get. Just tell them what happened to your mom, I'm sure they'll be—

MICKEY: *(Cutting her off)* Alright alright.

SAGE: Kyle Pearson told me having student loans is a modern day rite of passage.

MICKEY: Kyle Pearson said that, huh?

SAGE: Yeah.

MICKEY: Brilliant.

(Beat)

SAGE: So you drop off the face of the earth and now what do you want all of a sudden?

MICKEY: I don't know why you like that guy, Sage.

SAGE: What do you want, Mickey?

MICKEY: He's wears the same sweater vest everyday and dumb khakis and a belt with whales on it and his sweaters have stupid crisscross patterns on them.

SAGE: Did you just come here to make fun of my boyfriend?

MICKEY: No.

SAGE: So?

MICKEY: I don't know. I heard you were leaving today.

SAGE: How'd you know?

MICKEY: I asked around.

SAGE: Who?

MICKEY: No one.

SAGE: *(Exasperated)* Oh my God!

MICKEY: I saw your boyfriend at the Hess station, alright? I asked him when you were leaving and he said today and so I came over.

SAGE: Oh. He was here earlier.

MICKEY: I know.

(Pause)

SAGE: You know what's gonna happen to you?

MICKEY: What do you mean?

SAGE: If you don't go to college—or at least leave. You know what's gonna happen to you?

MICKEY: No. What?

SAGE: You're gonna stay here this year, then next year, then another year and another year until you're real happy working for Iggy Potzdale's dad until suddenly you're working for Iggy Potzdale who, if you'll recall, you punched in the face in the movie theater parking lot in tenth grade for calling me a slut.

MICKEY: Iggy's cool now!

SAGE: They're all gonna seem really cool really soon, Mickey!

MICKEY: No no you'd like him now—

SAGE: Mickey he still has a rat-tail and drinks Strawberry milk all the time!

MICKEY: Quit judging everyone, Sage.

SAGE: I— (*Small beat*) You're gonna get fat and mean and—and—and hairy and you'll watch T V and I'll come visit for Thanksgiving and—and—and—I'll—

MICKEY: What?

SAGE: I don't know!

MICKEY: You'll what, Sage? Go ahead and say it, you may as well, you've already said every other shitty thing you're thinking of plus you're disappearing in a few minutes so what difference will it make?

SAGE: I'll feel sorry for you!

MICKEY: Don't waste your time!

SAGE: (*Emphatic*) Then get out of here, Mickey! Get out of this town, now! Get to a city at least—it doesn't matter which!

MICKEY: I can't!

SAGE: Of course you can! I'm doing it!

MICKEY: You're different than me, Sage.

SAGE: How am I different from you? We're exactly the same!

MICKEY: No we're not.

SAGE: Of course we are! You're like my brother!

(MICKEY, *suddenly enraged, comes at* SAGE, *grabbing her by the arms violently.*)

MICKEY: Don't you fucking say that!

SAGE: *(Scared)* Mickey—

MICKEY: *(Half an inch from her face, fully enraged)* I'm not your fucking brother, Sage, alright? I am not your fucking brother!

SAGE: *(Nervous)* Okay—

MICKEY: You don't say that to Kyle Pearson, do you? Do you tell Kyle he's your brother? Huh? When you guys are in the backseat of his dad's fucking Prius? Do you tell him he's like your brother?

SAGE: No.

MICKEY: So don't say it to me!

SAGE: Okay. Mickey?

MICKEY: What?

SAGE: *(With strength)* Let go of me.

(Beat, MICKEY *does.)*

SAGE: *(Calmly)* I only said that because…I didn't mean anything by it.

MICKEY: Yeah right.

SAGE: I didn't.

MICKEY: You're braver.

SAGE: What?

MICKEY: That's how you're different than me, you're braver.

SAGE: I'm not braver. But I don't want what happens to people to happen to me.

MICKEY: What happens to people?

SAGE: *(With a gesture to him)* This!

(Beat)

MICKEY: *(Fuming, pacing)* You and Kyle gonna stay together?

SAGE: We're gonna try to.

MICKEY: Even at college?

SAGE: Yeah.

MICKEY: Huh.

SAGE: What's "huh?"

MICKEY: It's not like your Aunt Margaret's gonna be babysitting you anymore.

SAGE: What's that supposed to mean?

MICKEY: You could bring home any guy you wanted, right? Not that Margaret ever stopped you before.

SAGE: I have been faithful to Kyle the entire time we've been going out.

MICKEY: Give or take a night or ten.

SAGE: *(Turning on him, deeply insulted)* Get out of my yard.

(SAGE goes back to doing yoga. MICKEY feels like an asshole.)

MICKEY: Sorry. *(Silence)* Sage, I'm sorry. *(Silence)* Are you gonna ignore me now? I said I was sorry.

SAGE: You're not sorry. You're nasty and you're drunk all the time and now that you're not going to college you're also stupid. If you really need a job I know there's an opening for village caveman your dad left available.

MICKEY: Very funny.

SAGE: You'll excuse me if I ignore you.

(Beat as SAGE *continues her yoga, quickly hiding her face in a child's pose.)*

MICKEY: Hey Sage remember when we stole my gramma's fake mink coat with the mink heads still on it and we put it Wilma McEleny's mailbox? And she called pest control because she was so freaked out and pest control came and they had to use a giant fork to pull the mink out even though it wasn't a real mink? *(Silence)* Well do you?

SAGE: *(From her child's pose position)* Yes. That was mean.

MICKEY: You laughed. And remember when I dared you to eat some dry dog food and you did it and then you threw up in the bushes?

SAGE: *(Laughing despite herself, still in child's pose)* Yeah.

MICKEY: Remember when your mom bought that big thing of ketchup and we stole it and sprayed it all over the fence to reenact all Harvey's murders?

*(*SAGE *rises from her pose.)*

SAGE: My mom got so mad at me for that.

MICKEY: Yeah. You hear from her?

SAGE: Who?

MICKEY: Your mom?

SAGE: Oh. I talked to her about a month ago.

MICKEY: Oh.

SAGE: You ever hear from your dad?

MICKEY: No. My gramma talks to him sometimes, but I never do. *(Beat)* I didn't just come over outta nowhere. I've been planning to come over for a while.

SAGE: Really?

MICKEY: Yeah. And so when I saw Kyle at Hess and he said he was coming from your place I was like, finally he's not here, so I drove right over. I wanted to give you something before you left. *(He pulls out a small box from his pocket. It's got the vibe of a ringbox.)*

SAGE: *(Suspicious)* What's that?

(MICKEY chucks the box at SAGE, who catches it.)

MICKEY: Just open it, numbnut.

(Inside there is a shrunken Doritos bag, smaller than a credit card, on a key ring.)

SAGE: What is this?

MICKEY: It's a bag of Doritos.

SAGE: How'd you get it so small?

MICKEY: I shrunk it down in the oven.

SAGE: What?

MICKEY: You just put the bag in there at a super high heat and it shrinks. A bunch of 'em caught on fire before I finally got this one. It's Doritos 'cause I know you're all vegetarian now and you don't eat things that taste good. So this is kind of just to remind you how stupid you are.

(SAGE smiles, completely moved.)

MICKEY: You gotta put your dorm key on it, okay?

SAGE: Okay.

MICKEY: So when you bring some college frat guy idiot home with you, you think of me.

SAGE: *(Tearing up)* Okay. *(Beat. Through tears)* I'm not gonna do that, Mickey.

MICKEY: Yeah you will. It's okay.

SAGE: *(Crying)* Shutup.

MICKEY: It's okay.

(Small beat)

(MICKEY *and* SAGE *lock eyes. They then embrace one another primitively. They speak in the embrace.*)

SAGE: I'll be back for Thanksgiving, I promise.

MICKEY: You swear?

SAGE: I swear.

MICKEY: What if you don't have money for a plane ticket?

SAGE: I'll charge it.

MICKEY: Swear to God.

SAGE: I swear to God.

(*A car horn is heard.* MICKEY *and* SAGE *separate.*)

SAGE: That's Harvey. He's driving me to the airport.

MICKEY: That's nice of him.

SAGE: Yeah. He gave me some books to read on the plane, too. And a big box of his old records to bring. I didn't tell him I don't even have a record player. You wanna come for the ride?

MICKEY: I don't think so. Just text me when you land, okay?

SAGE: Okay. But you have to text me back.

MICKEY: I will.

(SAGE *heads for the exit.*)

MICKEY: Hey Sage?

SAGE: Yeah?

(SAGE *stands in the doorway.* MICKEY *looks at her.*)

MICKEY: Because you're wearing that red shirt and the wall behind you is red, you look like just a floating head right now.

(SAGE *begins to smile. Lights*)

END OF PLAY